e s
elow.
writing,
Service
due, b
online
and wil
or loss

Date

26. NO

Noah and the Ark
and Other Stories

Written by Anita Ganeri
Design and editorial by East River Partnership
Illustrated by Lucy Barnard
Series Consultant Roger Butler

Publisher Steve Evans
Creative Director Zeta Davies
Senior Editor Hannah Ray

Printed and bound in China

Noah and the Ark
and Other Stories

Anita Ganeri

Illustrated by Lucy Barnard

Noah and the Ark

There was once a man called Noah. Noah was a good man who loved God. He was always ready to do what God asked him to do.

4

But there were also many wicked people in the world. God was sad to see that the world was no longer a good place to live in.

God decided to send a flood of water to
wash the wicked world away. He told Noah
to build a big, wooden boat called an ark.
It would keep Noah and his family safe.

Noah and his family worked
very hard to build the ark.

It took years and years
and years. But at last
the ark was finished.

Then Noah and his family collected lots of
food and went into the ark. And every kind
of bird and animal also went into the ark,
two by two, a male and a female.

8

God sent a terrible storm. It rained and rained and rained for forty days and forty nights. The whole world was flooded with water.

When the rain stopped falling,
Noah sent out a dove. When
the dove came back with a leaf,
Noah knew that the ark was
near dry land.

Soon the ark came to rest, and Noah and all the animals came out. God sent a beautiful rainbow to fill the sky and life began again in the world.

The Birth of Jesus

Long ago, a woman called Mary lived in the town of Nazareth. One day, an angel told Mary that God had chosen her to have a special baby.

A powerful emperor ruled over the land. The emperor gave an order. He told everyone to go back to the town where their families came from. He wanted them to be counted.

Mary and her husband, Joseph,
had to travel to Bethlehem where
Joseph's family came from.

It was a long and dusty
journey. Mary rode on
the back of a donkey.

14

The town was crowded with people and there were no rooms to spare. The only place for Mary and Joseph to stay was a small stable.

Later that night, in the stable, Mary's son was born. She called him Jesus. She wrapped him in a blanket and laid him on a bed of soft straw.

16

On a nearby hillside, some shepherds were looking after their sheep. An angel told the shepherds that baby Jesus had been born and that he had been sent by God.

At once, the shepherds hurried off to Bethlehem. They took a tiny lamb as a present. There they found Mary, Joseph and baby Jesus.

Three wise men followed a star to the stable. They gave Jesus gifts of gold, frankincense and myrrh. They knew that baby Jesus would grow up to be someone very important.

19

Friends of Jesus

One day, Jesus was walking by a big lake.
He saw a fishing boat by the shore.
Jesus stopped to talk to the fishermen.

20

The fishermen were busy mending their nets.
It was hard work and it hurt their fingers.
They were glad to stop and rest.

The fishermen's names were Simon and Andrew. They had been out all night fishing, they told Jesus. But they had not caught a single fish.

Jesus told the fishermen
to row out again into the
middle of the lake. They
did not think it would do
any good. But they did
as Jesus said.

Simon and Andrew threw
their fishing nets over the
side of the boat. What
a surprise! The nets were
soon full of hundreds and
hundreds of fish!

One of the nets was so heavy, that the fishermen could not pull it up into the boat. They had never caught so many fish before.

Jesus was waiting when the fishermen got back to the shore. He told them to follow him so that they could help him to tell people about God.

26

So the fishermen left their fishing boats and nets, and went with Jesus. They became his special helpers and friends. They helped him to spread his message about God.

The Lost Sheep

Jesus often told people stories to teach them about God. One day, he told his friends this story of a little sheep that got lost.

Once there was a shepherd. He had a flock of one hundred fine sheep. He looked after them and kept them safe from wild animals.

29

One night, the shepherd was taking his sheep home. He counted them as they went through the gate. One, two, three…ninety-eight, ninety-nine…

One of the sheep was missing!
Where had it gone? The shepherd
was very worried. He set off to
look for the little lost sheep.

The shepherd looked
everywhere but he could
not find his sheep. Soon it
began to get dark. It was
difficult for the shepherd
to see anything.

Just then, the shepherd heard a sound. Baa! Baa! Baa! It was the sheep bleating. It had got tangled up in a nearby thorn bush.

33

The shepherd was so happy to see his sheep, he carried it all the way home. Then he had a party to celebrate finding his lost sheep again.

Jesus told people that
the shepherd in the story
was like God. God loves
and looks after everyone.
Everyone is special to God.

Notes for Parents and Teachers

About Christianity
Christianity began about 2000 years ago in the Middle East. Christians believe in one God who created and cares for the world. They follow the teachings of Jesus, whom they believe to have been wholly divine and wholly human. Jesus is known as the 'Christ', which means 'the anointed' or specially chosen one. They believe that Jesus is the Son of God sent to Earth to save people from their sins. During his life on Earth, Jesus taught people about God's love for them and showed them how to live according to God's wishes. Christians believe that Jesus died by being crucified but that, three days later, he rose from the dead. This is called the Resurrection. For Christians, it shows that death is not the end but the beginning of a new life with God.

About the stories in this book
In each of the world's religions, stories play an essential part. For centuries, they have been used to teach people about their faith in an accessible way, making difficult ideas and concepts easier to understand. For children in today's multicultural society, these stories also provide an ideal introduction to the different faiths, their key figures and beliefs.

Noah and the Ark
The story of Noah's ark is found in the Bible (Genesis 6–9). It deals with many themes, including obedience and making promises. God chooses Noah to take on the task of building the ark. Noah, despite any anxieties, does not hesitate in obeying God and putting his trust and faith in him. At the end of the story, God sends a rainbow as a sign of his promise to Noah that he will never flood the world again. The story also deals with trickier issues, including God's use of disasters to punish people.

The Birth of Jesus
The story of Jesus's birth is found in the Bible (Matthew 1–2; Luke 2). Every year, Christians remember this joyful time at the festival of Christmas. No one knows exactly when Jesus was born, but many Christians celebrate Christmas Day on 25th December. Many Orthodox Christians celebrate Christmas on 7th January. Christmas is marked with gifts, greetings cards, festive food and church services. Midnight Mass, which celebrates Jesus's birth at midnight on 24–25th December, is particularly important to Roman Catholics.

Friends of Jesus
This story is found in the Bible (Matthew 4; Mark 1; Luke 5). It tells how Jesus chooses his first disciples, his closest friends and followers. They are fishermen who take a great risk in giving up their livelihoods to follow Jesus and become 'fishers of men' instead. Jesus warns them that it will be a big commitment, and that they may face criticism and even persecution, but that God will help them. The word disciple means 'pupil'.

The Lost Sheep
This story is found in the Bible (Luke 15; Matthew 18). Christians believe that Jesus told the story to try to help people better understand what God was like. He wanted to show that God loves and cares for everyone, even if they are lost or unhappy. In the story, the sheep is lost because it strays away from the flock. Likewise, people can feel lost if they turn away from God. God is happy when even one person turns back to him, just as the shepherd rejoiced to have the one lost sheep back, even though he had 99 more.

Further things to do
• Read the stories out loud to the children. Talk about the stories with them. Ask them questions about what they think the stories mean. For example, why did God choose Noah to build the ark? How did Noah feel about that?
• Relate the stories to experiences in the children's own lives. For example, compare the birth of Jesus to the birth of a baby in their families, or the story of Jesus's friends to making friends of their own.
• Use a variety of different ways to tell the stories. The children could act out the stories, making masks and costumes for their characters to wear. Alternatively, you could make and use finger puppets from felt or paper.
• Decorate the classroom or home for Christmas. Encourage the children to make their own Christmas cards. Talk about the meaning of the special objects they see at Christmas. For example, the crib in a church. Extend this activity to look at other Christian festivals and the stories behind them.